To Parents and Special Educators:

Many children with an autism spectrum disorder (ASD) experience difficulties with daily life activities such as toileting. This activity can be especially difficult for those children who have sensory issues, and who lack body awareness. The purpose of life skills stories is to describe the experience in a step-by-step format in order to reduce the child's anxiety about the activity; life skills stories also state the behavior you expect from the child in a positive, upbeat way.

How to use a life skills story:

Life skills stories should be presented in a quiet and relaxed setting. Until the child becomes comfortable with the toileting routine, the parent should plan on reading the life skills story at least three times a day prior to toileting. By including the story in the daily routine, the child will know what to expect, and should become less anxious and more confident about this essential self-care activity. It is also extremely helpful to keep a toileting schedule so that the child has more opportunities to be successful. Supplementing the life skills story with other toileting books and videos will also reinforce the desired behavior. Although it is a matter of personal preference, toileting tends to go faster if the child wears regular underwear as much as possible rather than pull-ups.

Please note: It has been the authors' experience when working on toileting skills for boys with ASDs that it works best to start off sitting down to urinate. This may not be the case with your child, so try standing if sitting is not working out.

Spec the Autism Spectrum Puppy's Tips for Parents:

🐾 A sticker chart is a good incentive for toileting. Reward the child by allowing him to choose a sticker and place it on the calendar. Reward at first for performing the toileting routine, and then (once the routine is established), reward the child for voiding in the toilet.

🐾 Alternate rewards for toileting include small treats (such as candy, fruit, or chips) or an opportunity to play with a favorite toy that is designated as a potty reward toy.

🐾 Keep a basket of favorite books in the bathroom for your child to read while sitting on the toilet. This helps make toileting a more positive experience.

🐾 Offer your child fidget toys (such as a sensory ball or other fine motor type toy) to keep him busy while sitting on the toilet.

Ruff, Ruff!
Hi, my name is Spec. Everyone needs to go potty. Puppies like me potty outside. Big boys like you use the potty in the bathroom.
I'm very proud of you for using the potty. Thanks for being my friend! Woof!

Spec Tales: Life Skills Stories for
Kids with Autism & Special Needs

Going to
the Potty

for Boys

By Christine Ambrose
& Brenda Insalaco

Designed & Illustrated by Anna Myers

This book is for Dylan, Gabriel, Tyler, and Wyeth.

Spec Tales

Life skills Stories for Kids with Autism and Related Disorders

SPEC

TALES

www.spectales.com

Going to the Potty For Boys: ISBN: 978-0-9835317-3-9

Written by Christine Ambrose & Brenda Insalaco

Illustrated and designed by Anna Myers

BISAC Subjects:
JNF053180 JUVENILE NONFICTION / Disabilities & Special Needs,
JNF024110 JUVENILE NONFICTION / Health & Daily Living / Toilet Training

Spec Tales: Life Skills Stories for Kids with Autism & Special Needs

Going to the Potty

for Boys

By Christine Ambrose
& Brenda Insalaco

Sometimes I have to go
pee-pee and poop.

I need to use the potty to go
pee-pee and poop.

I need to tell Mommy or Daddy or my teachers when I need to use the potty.

I pull down my underwear,
and I sit on the potty.

Then I go pee-pee or poop.

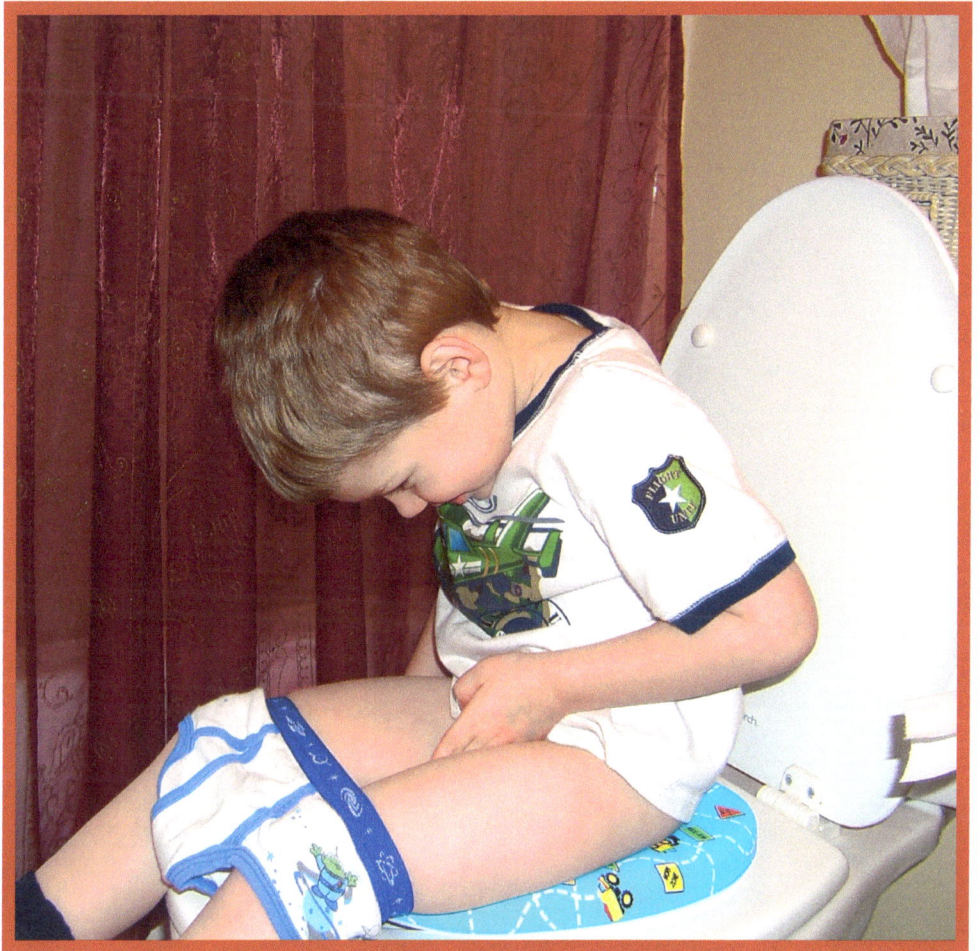

Sometimes I read a book when
I sit on the potty.

4

Sometimes I squeeze a toy while
I wait for the poop to come out.

5

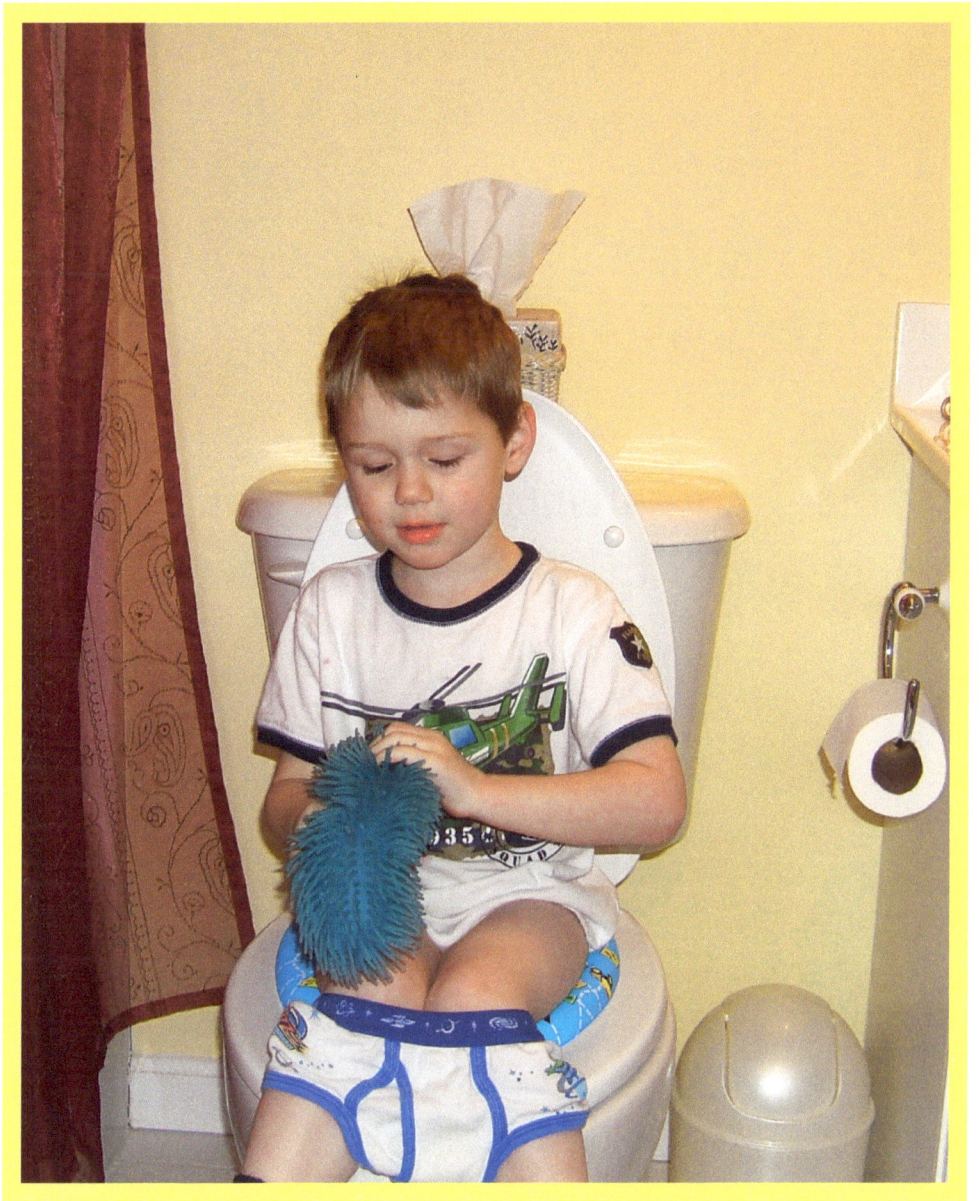

When I am finished peeing or pooping,
I wipe with toilet paper or wipes.

I flush the toilet, and watch the water go down.

Then I pull up my pants.

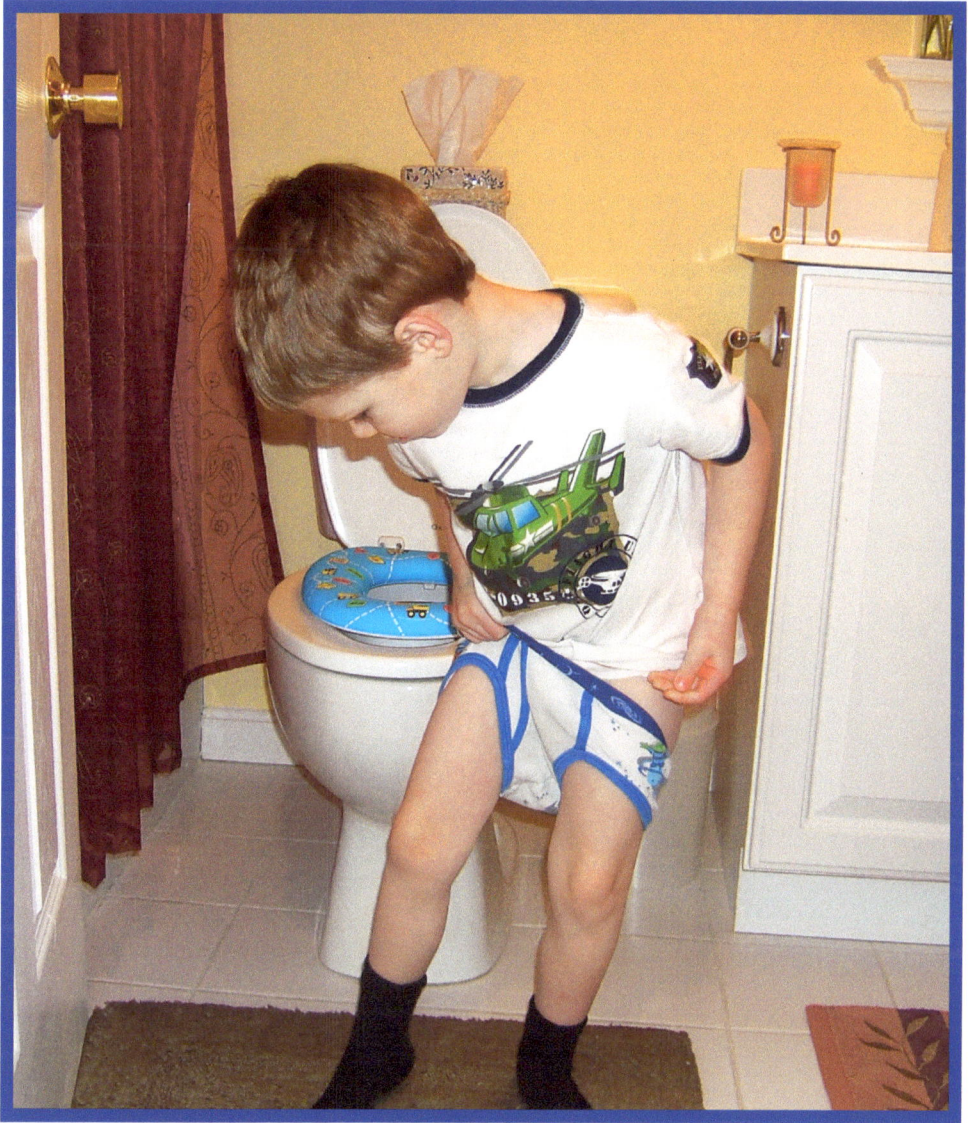

I turn on the water, and then
I wash my hands.

I use soap to wash my hands.

9

I dry my hands on the towel.

Then I get a sticker to put on the calendar.

Sometimes I get a different treat.

11

I am a big boy. I will use the potty to go pee-pee and poop.

12

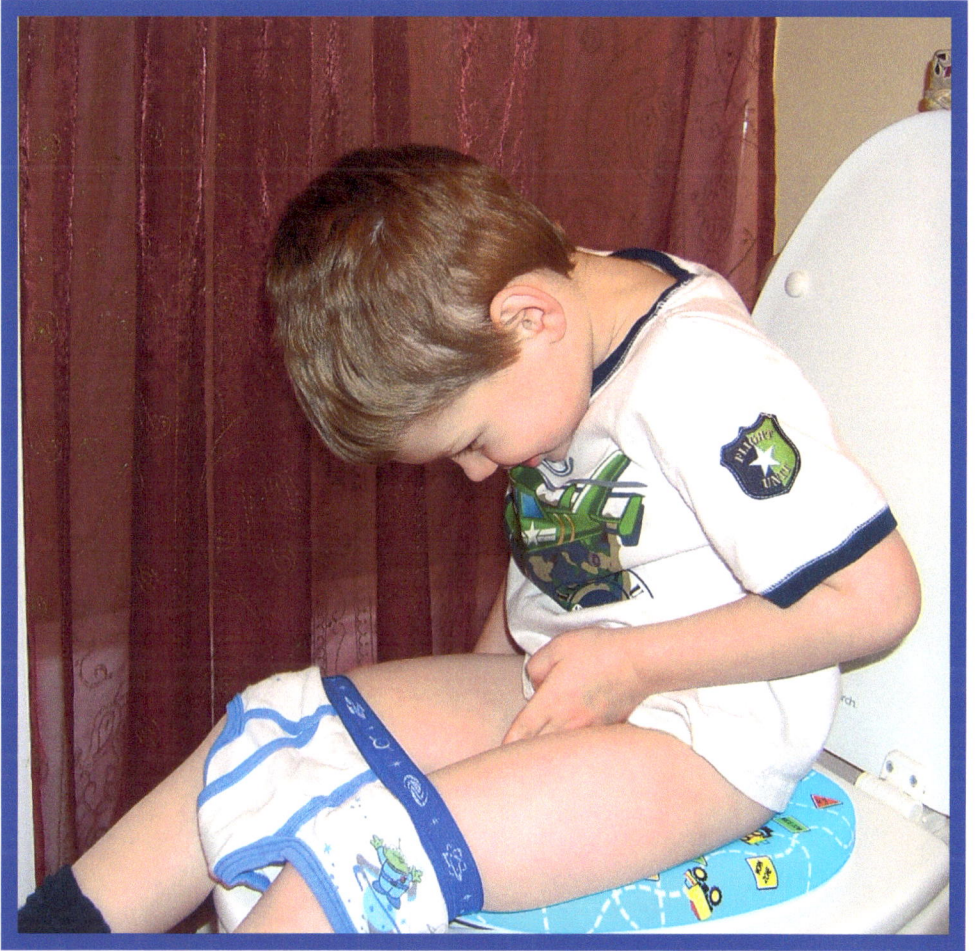

www.ingramcontent.com/pod-product-compliance
Lightning Source LLC
Chambersburg PA
CBHW041819040426
42452CB00001B/20